CUISINE
FEELING FOOD

Amr Muneer Dahab

authorHOUSE®

AuthorHouse™
1663 Liberty Drive
Bloomington, IN 47403
www.authorhouse.com
Phone: 833-262-8899

Published by AuthorHouse 07/06/2021

ISBN: 978-1-6655-3110-8 (sc)
ISBN: 978-1-6655-3109-2 (e)

To those who deal with food just as a means of survival,
to those who seek pleasure in food,
to those who regard food as a way of life and culture,
I hope they all find some inspiration in the book.

CONTENTS

PREFACE

This book aims primarily to inspire gastronomy and cooking passion in the reader, whatever his or her inclinations and skills in this regard.

A person increases and enhances skills in any work if he or she loves it, and if a person cannot love a job or a subject necessary for his or her life, then at least he or she must relieve their distress and discomfort to continue dealing with this work or subject in the best way.

Cooking, and food in particular, are of course indispensable for anyone. There are countless entryways to explore the splendor of gastronomy and to develop and enrich cooking skills and experiences.

Read *Cuisine* and create your own experience for a richer and more passionate relationship with cuisine.

STARTING FROM SCRATCH

1

Cooking is a talent that you can discover at any age. If circumstances did not allow you to cook for any reason in the past, this does not mean that you are a failed chef. Do not give up before you try repeatedly and give yourself enough chances to verify your talent and test your potential.

No matter how hard you practice or how far you take training courses, nothing matches passion if you aspire to become a great chef.

While passion is mostly evident from a young age, talent sometimes takes time to discover and needs the effort to cultivate. In any case, the passion itself grows with the acquisition of confidence in cultivating the talent.

The real start isn't the first time you've prepared a meal for a group of guests or even the first time you've cooked lunch for the family. It is the first time you had to go into the kitchen when you were young to prepare a small and extremely simple dish for your own breakfast or dinner.

It's okay if you get a little anxious or even fear failure in the very beginning. The problem is when you don't feel a deep joy transcending all other feelings every time you enter the kitchen.

Start with the easiest dishes you like, and beware of clinging to your comfort zone.

Even boiling eggs is an art: you must calculate the amount of water in relation to the number of eggs, temperature, and boiling time, in addition to your special touches, such as sprinkling some salt during the boiling, and the manner in which you serve the dish itself. When you do all this with passion, a connoisseur will be able to tell the difference between your eggs and those of a cook who threw the eggs in boiling water, took them out after a quarter of an hour, and pushed the dish to him or her.

It is good to offer the results of your first trials to people who are close to you and whose taste you trust. They won't put you down, so encourage them to openly give you their opinion to improve your next attempts.

Don't listen to common sayings. Less salt is not better than extra salt just because you can correct missing salt by adding the necessary amount. Ensure that you work with confidence. Do not leave it to the tasters to decide what is missing or excessive. Adjust the amounts of your ingredients with confidence and care, whether you always rely on a calibration tool or estimate amounts based on abstract senses.

It is never all or nothing. Cooking anything is better than never cooking. Even if you believe you lack the necessary passion or talent, do not stop learning and improving your skills. Instead prepare simple dishes that you prefer or that everyone around you likes.

PROGRESSING IN THE KITCHEN

2

Cooking is a talent; excellent training and continuous practice only reveal the talented chef. However, even if you lack innate talent, you can become a good chef if you are determined. Solid will and intense focus compensate for the lack of talent.

Your previous mistakes are your guidelines for your next try; pay attention to them, and try not to make new ones. This, of course, requires you to focus heavily on the first trial in order to extract the maximum possible lessons.

Cooking is an integrated process and not necessarily complicated in all cases. The taste is the most important in the end, but remember that the texture, the smell, and even the way of serving affect others' judgment of the dish, and these factors may sometimes cover up some minor taste slips.

Do not use a shortage of ingredients or poor materials as an excuse. A good chef will effectively wield his or her ingredients and control his or her materials, whatever they are, as soon as he or she decides to start working.

Low heat is essential for preparing a delicious dish. Cooking depends mainly on patience.

Pay attention to fine details. Sometimes the details have a fundamental role in the cooking process and important results on the served dish. If you leave the edges of the dough or pasta on the edge of the tray, they will burn. If you place the saucepan slightly to the side of a burner instead of in the middle, you will not have an even distribution of heat. If you add crushed rather than whole spices or nuts (or vice versa), the taste and texture of your dish will change.

The longer you work in kitchens, the more dishes you will learn to prepare, but even if you only learn a few dishes, the most important thing is that your experience should greatly increase your confidence and make you proud of the dishes you prepare.

A good chef never stops learning from everyone around him or her, not just from those who have more experience in the field. Even the chef's own mistakes should be a constant source of learning and inspiration for him or her.

The best way to advance your cooking skills is to make sure that you learn at least one new piece of information or cooking idea every day.

Sometimes you are disconnected from the kitchen or cooking certain dishes for a long time and feel you have forgotten everything. Don't worry. You will be able to fully restore your skills and more once you return to the kitchen and cook old dishes a few times.

Progress in the kitchen is not necessarily a matter of time; it is the result of passion and hard work.

Culinary secrets reveal themselves automatically when you sincerely and passionately embrace learning.

3 LEARNING TO TASTE

There are no hard rules regarding gastronomical experiences. As long as you are open to new experiences, your gastronomical skills will be continuously developed and enriched.

Try to avoid preconceptions before each gastronomic experience. Give your senses the chance to go through the experience as neutrally and impartially as possible and then decide accordingly.

In gastronomy too, the law of everything or nothing does not apply. Do not let an ingredient you do not like spoil the pleasure you derive from the rest of the ingredients of a delicious dish.

Always remember that taste experiences are not limited to the words *good* and *bad*. What you consider bad today may become good tomorrow and vice versa.

Taste is not fixed; it changes with age and experience. Every experience will open new horizons for gastronomy.

Tasting does not mean devouring. When embarking on a new taste experience, take a small piece, not with caution, but with eagerness to discover. You will not lose anything. If you like the taste, a new window has opened in front of you. If you do not like the taste, it may inspire a new idea or an amendment to an existing dish. In the worst case, you can completely forget the experience.

Expanding your taste is not just about trying new dishes or those prepared by a chef you are not used to. Taste is a passion that should be constant with every bite you eat, even if you are eating a dish you prepare yourself every day for breakfast.

The difference in tastes is self-evident, but this should not prevent you from listening to others' opinion or how they express their admiration for a taste you did not like. Their descriptions could make you change your mind or become less intense about a taste you did not like.

Connoisseurs taste food with all their senses, even if they are asked to do so while they are full.

If you don't find the taste you would expect in a dish you used to like, it doesn't necessarily mean that the ingredients or preparation methods have changed. You might have forgotten your memory of the taste, or the taste might have changed because of your mood. In any case, there is no problem. Taste is a world without limits. Be careful not to set restrictions that hold you back in this vast and enjoyable world.

If you missed your chance to become a professional chef, don't miss the opportunity to be a zestful gourmet.

Feel free to take advantage of every opinion on gastronomic experiences, but remember that your own opinion matters most. In the end, cooking is a matter of taste and does not have decisive laws of right and wrong.

BECOMING A PROFESSIONAL COOK

4

Of course, each piece of meat has its own cooking method, but the taste of the meat depends entirely on the chef's skill. A master chef can bring out the taste of a good piece of meat and conceal the taste of inferior meat through a charming combination of ingredients.

The most prominent sign you are becoming a professional cook is that you do not feel afraid or hesitant to cook a recipe for the first time because you are confident that the result will be acceptable at the very least.

Like an architect who knows the shape of a structure from its early design stages, a good chef feels absolutely confident about the taste and appearance of his or her food before preparing the recipe.

A good chef does not necessarily have to be an expert in raising livestock or growing crops, but he or she must necessarily be familiar with the whereabouts of good meat, vegetables, and spices, and he or she should be an expert in picking them.

You become a professional cook when you are no longer afraid to go into the kitchen to prepare whatever dish someone requests you, even if it were the first time to try preparing that dish.

Even a professional chef is not supposed to prepare all dishes of the same quality, but he or she must prepare everything requested from him or her satisfactorily and is not allowed to make obvious mistakes in the dish.

Every chef has his or her own personal style and behavior while cooking. But if you manage to merge vitality and calm, this will double the impression that you are a professional cook.

Being a professional cook does not mean that you memorize the ingredients and the way any food in the world is cooked by heart. The important thing is that you know how to deal with every cooking challenge you face, whether with the foods you know or the ones that are new to you.

For your professional cooking, it suffices to master the dishes that your kitchen specializes in, whether they are many or few. But at least make sure you familiarize yourself with what others offer outside of your kitchen. That will encourage and inspire you in one way or another.

Becoming a professional cook doesn't mean that everyone should like your cooking every time. But it is necessary that no connoisseur finds a clear flaw in your cooking at any time.

If we dare to go beyond the traditional judgments, the professional cook is a title that is sometimes deserved by some talented cooks under the age of ten or a little over. Experience matters, but talent surprises often exceed ages' expectations amazingly.

HOME COOK VERSUS PROFESSIONAL CHEF

5

🍳 Professional chef is a merit-related title and has nothing to do necessarily with the workplace. All of these may equally deserve the title: a housewife who lovingly prepares food for her family, an old man preparing food for inmates of an old inn, and an international chef in a five-star hotel.

🍳 You should be proud if you are a home cook. Home cooking preceded professional cooking by centuries.

🍳 Home-prepared food is not necessarily inferior to that which people eat in famous restaurants. The particular difference is that home food should essentially be prepared with love.

🍳 The traditional housewife cooking made with love and mastery continues to be a rich source of inspiration for the greatest professional chefs.

🍳 An international chef who supervises preparing food for hundreds of people in an international hotel needs a partner who lovingly prepares one dish for him or her to eat when he or she comes home exhausted at the end of the day.

Talent is not made in cooking schools. It is just discovered there. And when the talent is weak, the school brings out the best that can be brought out from the learner. Great talent develops itself through the means and tools available around it.

The home cook is usually experienced in specific varieties preferred by the family, but the original talent and great passion urge him or her to reach international standards between the walls of the home and its small kitchen.

Even if you are an excellent home cook, the challenge is not easy when you decide to become a professional chef. The issue is not related to mastering the culinary arts as much as it is related to other factors, but at the core of the professional work: cooking when asked and as required of you and not according to your own desire or mood, having the need to satisfy the customers' different tastes, making sure to present a wonderful dish that does not exceed the estimated cost of selling it, and so on.

A good home cook is in a state of constant passion to learn the newest in the arts of cooking. He or she is not content with anything less than mastery, whatever his or her circumstances and temperament.

There is a big difference between being a home cook and just cooking for the family. The second is a home task, while the first is a passion practiced at home in a professional spirit.

A professional chef cannot be a bad home cook, but he or she is very likely a lazy home cook.

MISTAKES IN THE KITCHEN

6

Whether the mistake was a result of negligence or completely inadvertent, the tension and breakdown will not help you. Take a deep breath and calm down even if it seems to you that you cannot do anything. In fact, you can always do something to correct the mistake or at least improve the situation and come out with the least losses in the served dish.

A good chef's ingenuity lies in his or her ability to correct mistakes no matter in any dish, even after it has been prepared. For a simple example, everyone can add the missing salt to the dish, but it is more difficult to deal with the excess salt.

Do not rush to name it a mistake before you think carefully about the possibility of using it to modify or improve the dish you are preparing and come out with a freshly created recipe.

A mistake only becomes a problem when it is repeated over and over. Even then, you don't have to stop working but rather think seriously about how to get past your repeated mistakes.

Fear of being wrong makes you wrong. If you think a lot about how to avoid mistakes, you probably need a short break to catch your breath and return to work with a new spirit.

Both a novice cook and a professional chef can make mistakes during cooking. But the mistakes of a professional chef should not appear in the dish when it is served, as his or her skills and experience should be manifested on the prompt attention to mistakes and quickly correct them during the cooking process.

Anxiety and rush are two main causes of cooking mistakes. What is the use of anxiety and rush? Leave them outside the kitchen threshold without thinking.

Your mistakes should not be a source of undermining your self-confidence in any way. Look directly for the cause of the mistake, not to justify to others, but to be able to best address it and avoid it in the future.

Focus is the magic word for avoiding cooking mistakes.

Take mistakes as a challenge and the way you treat them as an art.

Your understanding that mistakes are an essential part of work and your prior readiness to deal with mistakes keep them away from you at work and make you more confident.

YOUR MENTORS

7

See who inspired you to cook. You will find at least one person who gave you the confidence to start and still gives you the determination to keep going. This person does not necessarily have to be a good cook. He or she may be one of those close people who have always valued what you offer them with love and sincerity.

The best culinary mentors are not necessarily the best chefs. Teaching is generally an independent talent. In any case, make sure to take advantage of every opportunity to learn from everyone as you search for the culinary mentors having the best teaching capabilities and predisposition to inspire.

The good chefs you love will inspire you even better. But don't let your annoyance at some excellent chefs keep you from taking advantage of them and being truly affected by their inspiration.

With the specialized programs and platforms flooding cyberspace, you will never miss an answer to any question related to any recipe. It is wise not to exhaust your special relationship with your mentor in traditional questions. Instead make sure to passionately observe his or her cooking and listen carefully to the precious pieces of advice that spills over from him or her while at work.

There is no shame in dreaming of exceeding the capabilities and stature of your mentor. This does not imply any disrespect. There is no point in creating yourself a ceiling you fear or do not want to exceed for any reason. Unleash your potential and let it define your deserved stature.

In order to get the best of your mentors, make sure that your relationship with them is strong on a personal level, and do not make it appear as if it is limited to the interest of learning. This does not mean intruding on privacy; rather you should show sincere personal attention and honest stature appreciation.

The most important thing in evaluating an inspiring mentor is his or her unique cooking style, not necessarily the number of recipes he or she has created.

You do not have to act as if you were in a regular traditional school. Cooking is a world without limits, and your mentors are as many as you can find those who can benefit and inspire you in this exciting world full of adventures and challenges.

A good mentor should not keep some secrets of the recipe to himself or herself and divulge some of them. In any case, to appreciate the benefit you have gained from your mentor, do not count what you think he or she has withheld from you, but look at what you have already learned from him or her and what he or she inspired you.

While looking for the best mentor, don't just focus on the illustrious restaurant and hotel names he or she has worked for. The most important thing is not where he or she worked, but what he or she was doing there, wherever having a job opportunity.

A skilled experienced mentor explores your strengths and what you can excel at in your culinary future. But do not lose sight of the areas that did not arouse the attention of your mentor. You may have talents buried in these areas absent from even the most skilled professional mentors.

YOU AS A MENTOR

8

Do not despair of your junior cook, no matter how unpromising he or she seems to learn. He or she will come out at the end of the educational period better than he or she entered. The difference depends—bypassing the learner's personal abilities—on your patience and energy to inspire.

Teaching cooking does not necessarily mean looking for the mistakes of novice cooks to correct them. Deal with the dish prepared by your student neutrally, and give yourself the opportunity to savor it and discover any pluses or even creativity potentials before you start to comment on mistakes.

The most difficult cooking test for cooks is to let them observe how a dish is prepared and then ask them to prepare the same dish. It's like an open-book exam. Although implementation differs from observation, the skill here will not be demonstrated only in the craftsmanship of execution, but rather in the techniques and tricks that each of them must invent to show their uniqueness from the rest.

Like any inspirational mentor, encourage your pupils by highlighting their strengths and what distinguishes each of them. Talk about their weaknesses only to guide them on how to get rid of these weaknesses and thus build more confidence in their abilities.

As you teach your students a recipe, do not focus only on the ingredients of the recipe and the details of how to implement it. Make sure also to alert them to the tricks that benefit any chef during cooking in general and with regard to the techniques of that particular recipe alike.

Being a skillful and meticulous mentor does not mean being dry and rude. You can maintain and even increase your students' passion for cooking as you teach them the most complex cooking skills.

While you practice teaching cooking, do not miss the opportunity to benefit from your students, whether through the surprises of the rare talents' manifestations of those students or even out of their mistakes that will undoubtedly help you in one way or another in improving methods of communicating information to students in subsequent lessons.

As you direct your students to the ideal methods of cooking, be careful not to use the word *wrong* to describe methods of cooking you do not like or do not know much about.

Cooking in peace and tranquility is one of the most important features of a professional chef. This is something that is not indoctrinated, but rather is transmitted to your students through being a practical role model.

As you answer a question from one of your students, do not focus literally on the question he or she is asking, but try to get to the essence of what he or she is facing to open the way for him or her. The learners, especially the beginners, may get confused in the matter so that when they ask they cannot summarize or define the problem facing them.

It is not a shame to discover and acknowledge that your student possesses skills that surpass you in some aspects of cooking. The important thing is how you are persuasive and inspiring when you reveal to him or her what distinguishes you in the areas you teach him or her.

CROSS-CULTURAL COOKING

9

When you intend to merge different cuisines' flavors and before mixing two or several ingredients from each cuisine together, you must first be sure of the taste you are looking for and the senses you want to be tickled.

There is no dish in any culture that is not marketable outside of that culture, even internationally. Just be keen on what makes the local dish international by reducing the severity of the ingredients or processes that lead to the very sharp or very specific taste in that area, and keep the ingredients that can be acceptable to all. There is no objection to adding what can make the dish more widespread and acceptable without completely obliterating its local identity.

It is difficult to say that there is absolute singularity in food. No cuisine escaped being influenced by neighboring or distant cuisines. It should be noted that this is not a demerit but rather a feature that enriches every cuisine and dish anywhere in the world.

The secrets of any global cuisine fame do not just lie in secret recipes; they hide behind the complex styles of a rich culture and a substantial civilization.

Without the smart, broad, and intense promotion of your cuisine, people will not flock to it, no matter how rich in delicious food it could be. It is good to remember that a single dish with global success is enough to ensure that your cuisine becomes popular and ubiquitous.

Sometimes a country enters world cuisine through a single ingredient, not necessarily a complete dish.

Do not argue with people of a different cuisine and insist on convincing them of your point of view when you offer them a dish from their food culture that you have made some changes to. Instead try to understand what they didn't like in order to take advantage of that and make an improvement on the twist next time.

Whether you are introducing a dish from your local cuisine to the world or introducing from any cuisine in the world a dish to your local people, avoid literal copying and stay away from overmodification. Your ingenuity to maintain the identity of the dish lies in the simple twist that you must perform with precision and intelligence to pass the dish to people's hearts in the new cuisine.

You can learn a lot of cooking programs and even home cooks on various media. But wandering around and mixing with the owners of the original culture give you the necessary sense of creativity when you transfer any of their dishes to your own culture.

Regardless of the modifications and slight twists that can be made to dishes in the cuisines of other cultures, the presentation and serving approaches are magical introductions to the hearts of connoisseurs of the new culture.

It is not a crime if someone does not like food from another cuisine's culture or even if they only prefer the food of their own culture. But a professional chef has to accommodate any dish from any culture and know how to cook it with love, even if it is not one of his or her favorite dishes.

CROSS-CULTURAL TASTING

10

It is primarily a matter of a desire to open up. It is rare to like the food of any other culture if you come to it while you are fearing the experience or expecting a taste close to the food of your own culture.

This is what you should do every time, but especially when you are about to try food from a different culture for the first time, make sure you do not use your tongue only for tasting. You must approach the dish with an open mind and all of your senses before deciding whether or not you like the food.

When embarking on various gastronomic adventures, don't rely on common sayings and generic rules, such as a juicy piece of meat is better than a dry one. On the contrary, you are more likely to find yourself facing the challenge of accepting an experience that is totally different, or even contrary, to the taste, texture, and aroma of the food you are used to.

Trying the taste of food from different cultures is not in all cases an adventure you wish to end up with fewer losses, as you may get used to some of it sometimes to the point that you prefer it over the food of your own culture.

Do not be quick to judge negatively the cuisine of a different culture just as a result of one experience. The problem may be with an inexperienced chef from that culture, and the circumstances surrounding your first experience may be discouraging for more than a reason. Give yourself at least a second chance before you make a final judgment on that cuisine.

It is very rare to enjoy a food without understanding the culture it came out of. To get the most out of the flavor of a food, try to get to know and get closer to the culture that produced it.

In countries rich in ethnicities, the flavor of one of these ethnicities dominates its world-famous cuisine. Accordingly, a citizen of that country may face the same taste challenge like you as you both enter a restaurant bearing the name of his or her country, although you think he or she is supposed to be dealing with a familiar cuisine.

The tougher taste challenge you can face is not necessarily with the flavors of international cuisines, but it could be with foods you do not like and have to eat repeatedly from your own local cuisine by virtue of tradition.

Don't forget that the main idea related to your experiences with other cultures' food is taste, not satiety. Try to get as close as possible to the pulse of the other culture with each tasting experience and don't get caught up in thinking about whether you can fill your stomach with that food or not.

There is no reason to feel guilty or anxious. You do not have to love the food of another culture after trying it; nor do you need necessarily to continue to experiment. Keep your horizons open constantly and give yourself the opportunity more than once. You will inevitably find a suitable and pleasant way to express your opinion in front of others if you do not like the food. It is important to remember that no idea is devoid of a positive point of view, no matter what you do not like about it.

You can find at least one dish you will like in any kitchen around the world. Just try to get rid of prior impressions and eliminate prejudices as you enter any kitchen.

COOKING WITH LOVE

11

No one deserves the title of a professional chef unless he or she always cooks with love.

Cooking with love means both: love for cooking and love for those you cook for.

There's no need to worry. You don't intend to cook with love; it just happens automatically and spontaneously. But you must be in love with your work anyway.

A passion for cooking in the first place, and not necessarily your love for those you cook for, is what makes you cook with love.

Cooking with love stems primarily from the inside of the chef. But without a doubt, the appreciation of others deepens the chef's love while cooking.

A professional chef is interested primarily in the commercial success of his cooking. A chef who cooks with love is deeply concerned with the satisfaction of gourmets.

Cooking with love is nature, but smart coaching and wise mentoring sometimes succeed in stimulating that nature for some educated cooks who seem to miss it completely.

A chef who cooks with love teaches cooking also with love.

To make sure that food is cooked with love, you do not need to observe the chef while preparing it. You can certainly feel the food cooked with love while you eat it when it is served to you.

Cooking with love does not mean not making mistakes. However, in any case, a chef who cooks with love will not make obvious mistakes because his or her focus and ambition go well beyond merely escaping blame.

Cooking with love is not just about fun when you get to the kitchen. It's a subtle blend of love for the kitchen, happiness with every cooking experience, and a deep appreciation for the work you do.

EATING WITH LOVE

12

Eating with love does not mean swallowing cravingly; nor does it mean just savoring the taste. It's an integrated experience of deeply appreciating food, cooking, and even life as a whole.

A dish cooked with love will undoubtedly be eaten with love.

Tasting, no matter how subtle, does not go by itself to reveal the food cooked with love. Realizing the chef's feeling requires eating food with all your senses.

The strictest international standards of cooking cannot discover food cooked with love; it is only the chef's sense and the senses of those who eat the cooked food with all their hearts.

Professional food lovers know how to handle any food served to them, even if it is not prepared with the utmost care. In any case, they have the ability to focus on the positive and good aspects and not let the passing negatives spoil their enjoyment of food.

The fact that food lovers eat with all their hearts does not mean any sort of bypassing etiquette. On the contrary, eating with love includes the highest esteem for the etiquette of eating. We just have to remember that etiquette standards are relative.

Eating with love is not synonymous with eating a lot. It is primarily related to eating with all your heart and enjoying the different food experiences, regardless of the quantity available or amount you eat.

Eating with love is a natural trait; it can be detected at any stage of life and developed even as a skill. Take advantage of observing loyal food lovers and get inspired by their unique tendencies so as to awaken the food lover inside you.

Eating food with love gives you joy. It's rewarding and not as demanding as those who have a relationship of interest with food might probably imagine.

Eating with love is the greatest gift for those who cook with love.

If you missed eating with love, don't miss out on at least the grace of eating with gratitude.

HEALTHY FOOD

13

When it comes to healthy food, you should primarily pay attention to the amount served. Choosing the right ingredients and cooking healthily should not encourage you to eat what you crave without observing the amount.

Healthy cooking definitely raises the level of the gastronomic challenge. When a skilled chef works on preparing healthy dishes, he or she does not accept to sacrifice taste for the sake of health, but rather creates distinct flavors and unique tricks as compensation for the sacrifice of fats, sugars, and all their derivatives.

When you prepare a healthy dish, do not leave any opportunity for the gourmet to compare it with the original dish. Make your healthy dish unique as you sprinkle it with your own tricks to make up for the lost creaminess.

Healthy food primarily concerns nutritionists and those concerned with their health. The ingenuity of the master chef is to make these people savor and enjoy their healthy dishes so they forget it is specially prepared for health considerations.

A good chef meets the expectations of gourmets in general. The most difficult criterion that does not receive much attention is for a good chef to satisfy the expectations of those who request very special orders; this especially applies for preparing delicious, healthy food.

The secret to a healthy diet lies primarily in eating the right amount of whatever food is served to you. Healthy cooked food loses its meaning when you eat it up without counting.

Healthy food made with care and love needs connoisseurs with a particular taste sensitivity compared to gourmets in general.

When you have to stick to healthy food, do your best to enjoy the adventure of exploring new, unique, and developing savoring experiences.

Salt, sugar, and fats are not toxins; they are essential nutrients. Make sure to add these nutrients carefully and skillfully to your food so you can enjoy it throughout your life without interruption.

Fast food doesn't have to be synonymous with unhealthy food. You can prepare a healthy and delicious meal from a simple sandwich in a few minutes. To get a healthy snack, you don't need to overdo it with fat, salt, or sugar. Don't let stereotypes grab you. With some skill and genuine passion, you can get great taste in a few minutes.

Healthy food is a relatively recent term. It is not so much about food itself as it is about abundance and our modern lifestyles.

MOOD CHANGES

14

Mood change is natural over time, not only in what you prefer to eat, but also in what you like to cook.

Aging brings about a forced change in taste that doesn't call for any discomfort. Enjoy that. It is the divine harmony between the capabilities of your body and what is sufficient for your psychological gratification.

Take advantage of forced and sudden food mood changes to break out of the routine. It's okay to go back to some of your earlier favorite foods, and it's okay to try new foods you've been avoiding. The most important thing is that you try to create new foods that are especially inspired by these taste junctures.

While food mood changes appear to be a minor issue for gourmets, it is a valuable opportunity that a professional chef should not miss in order to think of some twisted or entirely innovated recipes.

🍳 Mild food mood changes occur every day, so it is not a good idea to keep a fixed weekly schedule necessarily for the items available for breakfast, lunch, and dinner.

🍳 Deliberate agile changes to your regular eating schedule are a preventative treatment for sudden food mood swings.

🍳 A simple side dish may satisfy the requirements of fleeting food mood changes.

🍳 You don't always have to think of complicated tweaks or tricks to deal with episodes of mood swings. Just changing the location, and the consequent slight change in the ingredients of the dish itself or the way it is prepared, can be enough to pacify and satisfy your fits of food mood changes.

🍳 The most difficult challenges related to food mood changes are those imposed by children.

🍳 Swapping items and dishes between meals is a smart idea to handle food mood swings challenges.

🍳 A slight change in the meal schedule is sometimes considered a tolerable ploy on food mood swings.

15

CREATING YOUR OWN STYLE

Mistakes, such as overlooking to observe cooking temperature or duration or forgetting to add an ingredient, are possible rich sources of inspiration. Stop grumbling when you are faced with one of these mistakes. Do not forget—while you are busy with attempts for correcting the fault quickly—to explore opportunities inspiring you to create an amended dish.

There is no right and wrong with cooking when it comes to creating flavors. Just make sure you know what you want from the new or twisted flavor, and constantly ensure to follow your strong and deep inner sense.

The ingredient that has not been tried before often appears strange and incongruous in the dish. Do not hesitate to add it if you feel a sudden urge to do so, as it might be the secret to creating a uniquely popular dish.

Don't be in a rush to invent your own style. As days go by and work hard, you'll find that your own style will automatically trickle down into your dishes as long as you are passionate about cooking.

Your own cooking style stems from yourself. As long as you work hard and honestly, don't bother proving that you are different from others in such-and-such.

Your style can't be reduced to just a unique dish. The special style is a charming and unique touch to every dish you serve.

The special style of cooking is necessarily accompanied by a special style of presentation. Both are best when they come automatically.

Flexibility is an important and effective quality in cooking and at every level in life. Feel free to make the necessary adjustments as you see fit and necessary to your own style. In fact, it is okay for your cooking style to change completely if the idea insists on you and you find a strong motivation stems from within you toward a new style for a new stage of your career.

With your own style, you are not in competition to see who is the best. The important thing is that your style should emerge from your very own experience to automatically acquire its own distinctive features, regardless of being better or worse than other experiences.

One's own style is not a final destination beyond which the chef does not advance. You have to constantly work on your own style in order to show it best and make it flexible for each situation and occasion.

Your cooking style is the culmination of your passion and hard work. Present it to others with love and appreciation, away from ostentation and vanity.

FOOD FREEDOM

16

🍳 In food, there is no right and wrong so much as there should be a connoisseur who is open to all gastronomic experiences.

🍳 When we talk about food freedom, we talk about open horizons and limitless possibilities for creativity.

🍳 While a good cook has the freedom to cook any food item that comes to his or her mind, this freedom does not mean that he or she should not be ready in return to cook any food item that is asked of him or her, even if he or she does not like that item.

🍳 Food freedom does not mean underestimating quality, noting that quality in no way means high cost as much as it means adherence to the best standards according to the available budget.

🍳 While some extreme conditions could be an incentive to dare to your unpreferred food list, the best way to experience the food you don't like is unique culinary places with good company.

The food you adore needs no justification, and neither does your unfavorite food. Just do not hesitate to try the latter whenever you have a different opportunity, as this may constitute a wonderful reconciliation that enriches your feelings and food culture, unlike what you expect.

Your love and pride in your patriotic food should not be an obstacle to your appreciation for the food of other cultures.

The toughest food freedom challenges you face are with children.

You have the right to express your personal opinion about any food, but it is not wise to denounce a particular dish just because you did not realize the story behind its creation.

The adventurous chef has the right to try to cook any food that strikes his or her mind, but the secret of success is not so much in random experimentation as in the chef's deep faith in every step he or she takes in his or her work.

Food freedom is more about free spirit than it is about the love of food.

FOOD FASHIONS

17

It is not only the cooking methods and techniques that are subject to the influence of fashion and trends, but also the prevalence of the different types of vegetables, fruits, nuts, drinks, and more.

There is not supposed to be a single sacred food menu in any place from which one can choose. We can create whatever dishes we want and add them to the menu of any cuisine as long as we are passionate, daring, and appreciative of the cuisine we deal with.

Fashion in cooking doesn't just mean that an innovative food has met with unrivaled success. It could happen with an old dish that is being revived.

The food fashion that sweeps the markets and enters every home is not often about inventing an unprecedented flavor. It is mainly a matter of rare luck crowning a thoughtful marketing and a smart promotion.

Traditional local food is the richest source of inspiration for international cuisine's food trends. That does not require more than slight adjustments occasionally and a unique promotional intelligence necessarily.

Personal financial distresses and common acute crises in resources and food are excellent opportunities to create affordable dishes. Seize these opportunities with patience and cleverness to innovate simple food trends rather than just complain.

Mixing any random ingredients will not lead to the invention of a successful new food trend unless it is accidentally done through a rare chance. Deliberately inventing new successful food trends requires experience, skill, effort, and patience crowned ultimately with great luck.

The master chef puts his or her own touch on every dish he or she prepares, but he or she doesn't necessarily invent a new dish. Invention of a new food fashion requires a passion that goes beyond mastering high-tech skills in cooking, and it is at times just a matter of luck.

Nobody can say for sure which dish will become a hit in advance. The trending dishes like anything successful; it is easy to talk about why it works only after it has been achieved.

Transferring food from one country's cuisine to another is a good source of inspiration for a trendy dish. Just beware of literal copying. Pay attention to the subtle changes needed to endear the chosen dish in the new country's cuisine.

When trying to create new, trendy food from an old dish, this does not necessarily require changing an ingredient or adding a new one. The smart trick might be to just eliminate an ingredient in the old dish or even cancel a stage in the classic cooking process.

THE SOUL OF CUISINE

18

What is called the "chef's spirit" in cooking is not magic or a secret. It is a combination of several skills that are the result of talent and passion: constant glowing desire, intensive focus, attention to details and eagerness to implement them, high confidence, mastery, openness to flash ideas' manifestations and daring to assimilate them, and so on.

The soul of cuisine is one, but every people, ethnicity, region, family, and house has its own style and flavor in the kitchen.

You touch the soul of cuisine when you do not hesitate to enter any kitchen around the world with respect, appreciation, a sincere desire to learn, and a passionate taste.

The soul of cuisine accommodates every dish prepared with ingenuity and passion, whatever its taste.

Learning to cook may mean copying when it comes to a single recipe. But the title of an excellent cook is only deserved by getting to the soul of each recipe.

When cooking soul possesses the chef, he or she does that automatically, but there is nothing wrong with paying special attention to the harmony and mixture of colors and aroma with the nature of the dish to be served.

The tongue is the taste organ for every human being. As for a gourmet, he or she depends on his or her five senses and soul in any gastronomic experience.

Perfect cooking doesn't mean more ingredients or complicated processes. The fewer ingredients and simpler cooking processes will not prevent the soul of cooking from creeping into a lovingly crafted dish.

The soul of dealing with food is not only embodied in the passionate chef while he or she cooks, but also in the master gourmet as he or she tries any dish served to him or her, as well as in the loyal food lover while he or she listens to any recipe in any session devoted to talking about food or even during a casual chat.

The sound soul of dealing with food will never be stuck with a new ingredient or an exotic flavor when trying any cuisine for the first time anywhere in the world.

The individual reaches the deepest level of the soul of gastronomy when all barriers fall in front of him or her regarding worldwide cuisines, so that he or she does not see in any cuisine except the unique flavor that distinguishes the cuisine and what is behind it of a special culture and a unique passion.

Printed in the United States
by Baker & Taylor Publisher Services